EARTH, SPACE, AND BEYOND

HOW DO SCIENTISTS
EXPLORE SPACE?

Robert Snedden

Raintree

Chicago, Illinois

EXPRESS EDITION

www.capstonepub.com
Visit our website to find out more information about Heinemann-Raintree books.

To order:
☎ Phone 800-747-4992
🖳 Visit www.capstonepub.com
to browse our catalog and order online.

Edited by Andrew Farrow, Adam Miller, and Adrian Vigliano
Designed by Marcus Bell
Original illustrations ©Capstone Global Library 2011
Illustrated by KJA-artists.com
Picture research by Hannah Taylor
Originated by Capstone Global Library Ltd.
Printed in the United States of America in North Mankato, Minnesota.
022013   007209RP

15 14 13
10 9 8 7 6 5 4 3

Library of Congress Cataloging-in-Publication Data
Cataloging-in-Publication Data is on file at the Library of Congress.

ISBNs: 978-1-4109-4176-3 (HC) 978-1-4109-4182-4 (PB)

Acknowledgments

The author and publishers are grateful to the following for permission to reproduce copyright material: Corbis pp. 4 (©Reuters/ HO), 16 (©REUTERS/NASA-Johns Hopkins University Applied Physics Laboratory/Carnegie Institution of Washington), 19 (©kyodo/XinHua/Xinhua Press), 20 (©Reuters), 28 (©Reuters TV), 31 (©NASA), 36 (©NASA/ STScI), 37 (©NASA/ STScI), 38 (©epa); Corbis SABA p. 9 (©Najlah Feanny); Getty Images p. 5 (amana images); ©Justin Knight p. 33; NASA pp. 8, 12 (JPL), 13 (JPL-Caltech), 14, 18 (JPL), 21 (JPL-Solar System Visualization Team), 22, 23, 29, 30, 32 (ESA/ G.Bacon), 34, 40 (PIRL/University of Arizona); Science Photo Library pp. 6, 7 (©European Space Agency/ DLR/ Fu Berlin [G.Neukum]), 10 left (©Gemini Observatory/NOAO/ AURA/NSF), 10 right (©NASA), 24 (©European Space Agency), 25 (©European Space Agency), 26 (©NASA), 39 (©Walter Myers); SETI p. 41; Shutterstock p. 15 (© Christian Darkin).

Cover photograph of astronaut in space reproduced with permission of NASA.

We would like to thank Professor George W. Fraser for his invaluable help in the preparation of this book.

Every effort has been made to contact copyright holders of any material reproduced in this book. Any omissions will be rectified in subsequent printings if notice is given to the publisher.

EARTH, SPACE, AND BEYOND

HOW DO SCIENTISTS EXPLORE SPACE?

Contents

Sky Watchers 4

Project Planet 12

Comet Encounters 24

Solar Explorers 28

Other Stars, Other Worlds 32

Being There 38

Timeline of Space Exploration 42

Glossary 44

Find Out More 46

Index 48

Some words are shown in bold, **like this**. You can find out what they mean by looking in the glossary. You can also look out for them in the "Word Station" box at the bottom of each page.

Sky Watchers

The earliest space explorers looked up at the night sky. They wondered about what they saw. These were the beginnings of space exploration. All it required was sharp eyes and curious minds.

Scientists study many parts of space. They look at huge columns of dust like these.

WORD STATION
astronomy scientific study of space

Astronomers imagined patterns connecting stars. These patterns are called constellations.

Navigation

The patterns of stars in the night sky are called **constellations**. Astronomers labeled the constellations a long time ago. Modern astronomers still use constellations as an easy way to describe the night sky.

Fixed stars

The first sky watchers noticed something. Most objects in the sky rose and set in patterns. These patterns always stayed the same.

Wandering stars

These sky watchers also noticed some objects that did *not* follow regular paths. Thousands of years ago, in the country of Greece, people called these objects *planetes*. This means "wanderers." This word is where we get the English word "planet."

All of these early observations became the basis of modern **astronomy**. This is the study of everything in space.

Aristarchus

Aristarchus was a Greek **astronomer** who lived about 2,200 years ago. (Astronomers are scientists who study space.) He correctly figured out that the Sun was much bigger than Earth. He also believed that Earth moved around the Sun. It would be almost 1,800 years before that idea was accepted as fact.

Where are the Martians?

U.S. astronomer Percival Lowell (1855–1916) studied the planet Mars through telescopes. He thought he saw stretches of water across Mars. He was sure that intelligent creatures had built and used these stretches of water. Soon the idea of walking, talking creatures—or "Martians"— became popular. But in 1965 the spacecraft Mariner 4 reached Mars. It proved that Mars was an empty planet, with no life.

The telescope

Space exploration took a great leap forward with the **telescope**. The scientist Galileo Galilei (1564–1642) built one of the first telescopes in 1609. It allowed him to see things in the night sky that were very far away. Compared to modern telescopes, it was not very powerful. But Galileo used it to discover mountains on the **Moon** and spots on the Sun.

Galileo also discovered that the planet Jupiter had small, rocky objects (moons) circling around it. At that point, people thought that everything in space **orbited** (circled around) Earth. The moons of Jupiter showed that this was not the case.

Percival Lowell drew this sketch of Mars. He thought intelligent creatures made these paths of water.

WORD STATION
orbit circle around something, such as a planet

Limits to seeing

Over the next 300 to 400 years, telescopes kept getting bigger and better. **Astronomers** kept making new discoveries about the **universe** (space and everything in it). But there were limits to what they could see. This is because of the layer of **gases** that surrounds the planet, called the **atmosphere**. (A gas is a substance with no shape, like air.) The atmosphere was preventing astronomers from getting a clear view of space.

The Mars Express spacecraft took this photograph. It shows an ancient riverbed on the planet Mars. There has not been any water on Mars for billions of years.

Telescopes in space

In 1990 scientists solved the problem of the **atmosphere**. They sent a **telescope** beyond Earth's atmosphere—into space! This was the Hubble Space Telescope. It was sent by the U.S. space agency, the **National Aeronautics and Space Administration (NASA)**.

This shows the Hubble Space Telescope.

WORD STATION
National Aeronautics and Space Administration (NASA) U.S. space agency

Hubble Space Telescope

After the telescope was in space, scientists need to fix problems with its main mirror. Then, Hubble was able to send pictures back to Earth. The results showed amazing images of the **universe**.

A number of **missions** have returned to Hubble. A mission is a space program with a specific goal. These missions have replaced parts that have failed. They have also kept its equipment up-to-date.

Even so, a replacement for Hubble is planned. The James Webb Space Telescope is already being prepared for use in 2014. More than 1,000 people in 17 countries are currently developing it. (See the box above right for more information.)

James Webb Space Telescope

The James Webb Space Telescope will have a mirror that is 6.6 meters (21.7 feet) across. (Hubble's main mirror is less than half that size.) Getting a mirror this big into space is a challenge. The Webb team came up with a design using 18 six-sided pieces. These pieces are made of a material that is light, yet strong. The pieces will be folded up to fit inside the rocket **launcher**. A launcher is a vehicle that carries something into space. Once the telescope is in position in space, the mirror will unfold. Observations can then begin.

Dr. Heidi Hammel has made excellent use of the Hubble Space Telescope. She has studied the planet Jupiter and other parts of space.

Looking beyond light

Why can we see things in space? It is because light from these objects reaches us. Visible light is a type of **energy**. (Energy is the ability to do work.) It is given off by objects in space.

But objects in space give off other types of energy, too. In fact, a range (variety) of energy types travel through space. This range is called the **electromagnetic spectrum**. All these types of energy travel in **waves** (invisible paths of movement).

Radio astronomy

Scientists use these waves to learn about parts of space. For example, the longest waves of energy are called **radio** waves. **Radio telescopes** work by picking up radio waves. These waves—and telescopes—let scientists look at far-off, dusty parts of space.

These are two views of the planet Jupiter. On the left it appears as an infrared image. On the right it appears as an X-ray image.

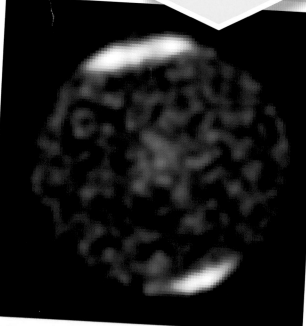

WORD STATION
energy ability to do work

Infrared astronomy

We cannot see **infrared** waves. But we can feel them as heat. The warmth of the Sun comes from infrared waves. Very few infrared waves reach the surface of Earth. But scientists can use **telescopes** in space that pick up infrared. One example is the Spitzer Space Telescope (see page 33).

X-ray astronomy

Gamma waves and **X-rays** are waves with a lot of energy. Very hot objects in space, such as exploding stars, are the main source of these waves. Again, these waves do not usually reach Earth. So, these must be picked up by special **instruments** (pieces of equipment) sent into space. By studying these different kinds of waves, scientists get a fuller picture of what is in space.

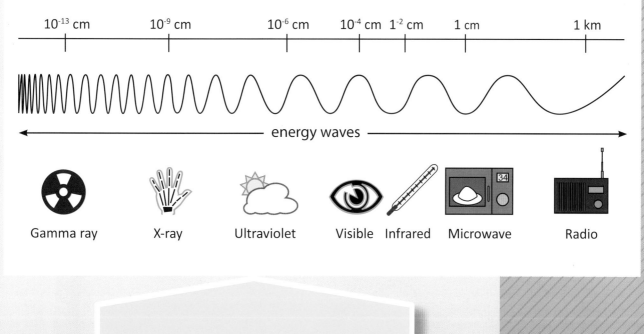

The electromagnetic spectrum is the range of energy that travels through space. Energy travels in the form of waves.

Project Planet

Some scientists are interested in how objects in space, such as planets, were formed. They also study how these bodies continue to be shaped today.

Up until the middle of the 1900s, all of these investigations were carried out with **telescopes**. But everything changed with space **probes**. Probes are spacecraft that are sent into space. They can perform experiments without people.

This is a photograph of the planet Mars. It was taken by the space probe Mariner 4. This was one of the first images of another planet to be sent back from space.

WORD STATION

probe spacecraft that carries instruments for research, but not people

This image is an artist's idea of what Voyager 1 looks like in space.

Voyager's journey

One of the most successful probes is NASA's Voyager 1. In 1979 and 1980, it took images of the planets Jupiter and Saturn, as well as their **moons**. Thirty years later, Voyager is farther from Earth than any other probe. It continues to send back information about the solar system. Scientists expect Voyager to keep working until at least 2025.

First probes

The first space probe to reach another planet was **NASA's** Mariner 2. It flew near the planet Venus in 1962. Since then, a huge number of probes have studied our **solar system**. This is made up of all of the major planets and other objects that **orbit** the Sun. Space probes have provided incredible details. This information could never have been possible with telescopes alone.

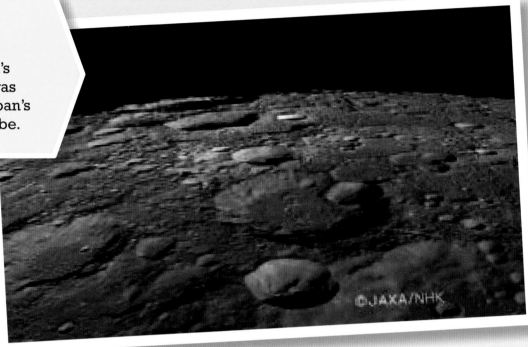

This is a photograph of the Moon's surface. It was taken by Japan's Kaguya probe.

©JAXA/NHK

From the Earth to the Moon

The closest object to Earth in space is the **Moon**. It is the brightest object in the night sky. It is also the only other place in the **universe** that people from Earth have visited.

Project Apollo

Between 1969 and 1972, Project Apollo first landed people on the Moon. Apollo was a space program run by **NASA**. The **mission** brought samples of rock back to Earth. By examining these rocks, scientists learned that the Moon has always been lifeless. Studying the rocks also revealed the history of the Moon. The Moon developed after another object smashed into the young Earth. This crash threw huge, broken pieces into space. These pieces gathered together to form the Moon.

Over millions of years, rocky objects called **asteroids** and **meteorites** pounded into the Moon. The surface of the Moon is covered in a layer of dust and rocks left by those crashes.

WORD STATION
asteroid rocky object orbiting the Sun in the solar system

Robots to the Moon

The countries of India, China, and Japan have all successfully sent **probes** to the Moon in recent years. Japan is currently developing plans for a **base** on the Moon. A base is a permanent location that can be used over time. The base will be operated by robots!

The first robots are scheduled to arrive on the Moon by 2015. They will roam around the Moon's surface. The robots will collect samples to be sent back to Earth by rocket.

The next stage is for the robots to build a Moon base by 2020. At that point, **astronauts** (people who travel to space) might join the robots. Japanese scientists believe that a Moon base will be an important starting point for exploring the **solar system**.

This image shows how the robot-operated Moon base might look.

meteorite space rock that crashes onto the surface of a larger object in space

Messenger to Mercury

Mercury is the closest planet to the Sun. So far, only two spacecraft from Earth have visited Mercury. The first craft to reach Mercury was **NASA's** Mariner 10. This was a **probe** launched (sent into space by rockets) in 1973.

Mariner 10 made use of something called a **gravity assist**. This involves passing a probe by a planet. It has to be done at just the right angle. At this angle, the planet's **gravity** affects the probe. (Gravity is the pull that a large object has on a smaller one nearby.) The planet's gravity has a big pull. This pull can be used to change the speed and direction of a small probe. Mariner 10 used Venus's gravity to slow down on its way to Mercury. This saved rocket fuel.

The surface of Mercury was photographed by MESSENGER.

WORD STATION

gravity pull that a large object has on a smaller one nearby

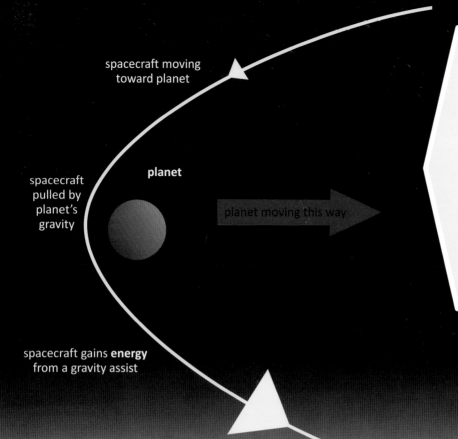

spacecraft moving
toward planet

planet

spacecraft
pulled by
planet's
gravity

planet moving this way

spacecraft gains **energy**
from a gravity assist

An approaching spacecraft is pulled toward a planet by the planet's gravity. At the correct angle, the craft can use the planet's gravity. It can use it to change direction and speed. This saves valuable rocket fuel.

MESSENGER

NASA's MESSENGER (the MErcury Surface, Space ENvironment, GEochemistry, and Ranging) spacecraft is a **satellite**. A satellite is an object that **orbits** a planet. The MESSENGER will enter orbit around the planet Mercury in March 2011. It will be the first satellite to be placed in orbit around this planet.

The Mercury Dual Imaging System (MDIS) is an **instrument** that will be carried on board MESSENGER. The MDIS will help scientists study the different types of rock on Mercury.

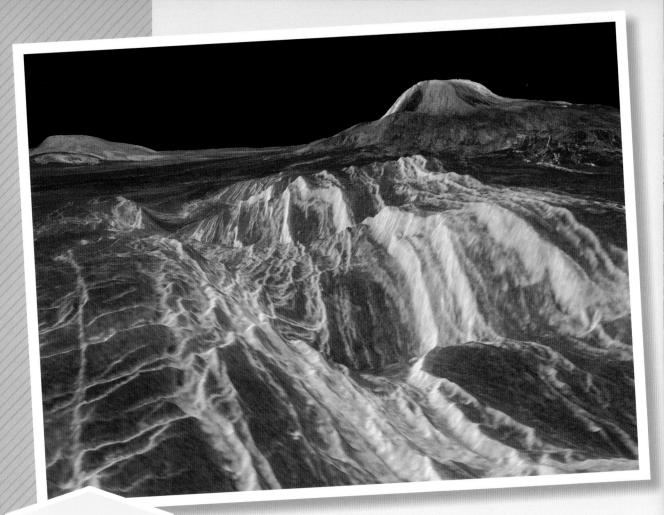

This image is of the surface of Venus. It was taken from the Magellan space probe.

Venus weather watch

We are used to seeing reports of the weather here on Earth. The information used in these reports comes from **satellites**. Now there is a **mission** to take a look at the weather on another planet.

Akatsuki

The Japanese space **probe** Akatsuki was built to study the weather on the planet Venus. Strong storm winds blow across the surface of Venus. On board Akatsuki are **infrared** cameras. These can peer through the thick **atmosphere** of Venus. They can see the surface of the planet. It is hoped that they might reveal the cause of the high-speed winds.

WORD STATION
infrared waves of energy that travel through space; we feel them as heat

Akatsuki was first launched on May 21, 2010. It was scheduled to enter **orbit** around Venus in December 2010. This first attempt failed. But it is hoped that it will enter Venus's orbit in the future.

Satellite partnership

If Akatsuki reaches Venus, it will join a **European Space Agency (ESA)** spacecraft called Venus Express. This is already in orbit around Venus. It studies the planet's atmosphere.

The two different space agencies plan to work together. By combining their discoveries, they hope to learn more about Venus.

A rocket carrying the Akatsuki space probe lifts off from Japan.

Red planet rovers

Scientists have sent a number of **probes** to explore other planets and the **Moon**. Space vehicles called **landers** land on the surface of these new places. They then release vehicles called **rovers**. Rovers travel across the surface. Two of the most successful rovers have been **NASA's** Mars Exploration Rovers. They are called Spirit and Opportunity.

Martian mission

The Mars rovers arrived on Mars in January 2004. Their main **mission** is to sample a wide range of rocks and soils from the surface. Scientists have found evidence that water once flowed on Mars. This water might have made it possible for life to exist on Mars long ago.

This artwork shows one of the Mars Exploration Rovers on Mars.

WORD STATION
lander space vehicle that lands on the surface of an object in space

This shows a sunset on Mars. The Sun appears smaller than it does on Earth. This is because Mars is much farther from the Sun than Earth is.

Setting a course

When the rovers first arrived on Mars, they took full-view pictures of their surroundings. This helped scientists on Earth choose places that seemed worth investigating on Mars. At the start of each day, a set of instructions is sent to the rover. These instructions tell the rover where to go. It also orders what tests to carry out.

Avoiding hazards

The rover has computer programs that help it avoid danger. Every few seconds, the rover stops and examines the surface in front of it. It uses a pair of special cameras. If there is a possible danger ahead, the onboard computer will instruct the rover to change its path.

Rover update

The Mars rovers have kept going far longer than scientists expected. By summer 2010, Spirit had lost power and lost contact with Earth. Scientists hope to regain contact when it recharges. It will recharge using **solar panels**. Solar panels take in and use the power of the Sun. Opportunity continues to send back information.

Juno to Jupiter

The planets are not unchanging objects. For example, the **Southern Equatorial Belt** is a group of clouds circling around the planet Jupiter. It is more than twice as wide as Earth. Yet every now and then, it vanishes. It then mysteriously reappears when storms circle Jupiter.

Scientists would love to know why this happens. Scientist Glenn Orton thinks that changing wind patterns on Jupiter are the cause. They have caused some clouds to form and cover up the cloud belt. But no one can explain why the southern belt should vanish, while the northern belt remains.

These photographs show that Jupiter's Southern Equatorial Belt of clouds has disappeared.

Jupiter

Before
Aug. 4, 2009

After
May 8, 2010

WORD STATION
Southern Equatorial Belt group of clouds circling around the planet Jupiter

Juno

NASA's Juno **probe** may provide some answers. Juno has special **instruments** that will study Jupiter. It will measure things like Jupiter's strong **gravity**. It will look at Jupiter's **atmosphere**. Juno is going to be launched in August 2011. It will take Juno five years to get from Earth to Jupiter.

Comet Encounters

The Kuiper belt

Astronomer Gerard Kuiper studied the paths followed by many comets. In 1951 he said there must be hundreds of millions of comets beyond the planet Neptune's orbit. This group is now known as the **Kuiper belt**.

Comets are icy remains. They are left over from when planets formed. Comets **orbit** the Sun. As they do so, some comets come very close to the Sun. The Sun's **energy** then heats them up. This causes **gas** and dust to boil off of the comets. This forms the tail that streams behind them.

Rosetta

The **ESA's** Rosetta **probe** will explore a comet at close range. It is on its way to meet with Comet 67P/Churyumov-Gerasimenko in 2014. When it arrives, the probe will go into orbit around the comet. It will spend the next two years following the comet. It will follow it as it heads toward the Sun. A small **lander** will also be placed on the surface of the comet. A number of experiments will be carried out.

The Rosetta probe leaves Earth. It is on its way to meet with a comet.

Opposite page: An artist has imagined how Rosetta might look on the comet's surface.

WORD STATION
comet fairly small, icy object that orbits the Sun

Comet approach

It is important for Rosetta to get on the same path as the comet. As Rosetta nears the comet, it will fire its braking rockets. Rosetta will slow to match the comet's speed. Eventually, if all goes well, it will enter an orbit just 25 kilometers (16 miles) above the comet's surface.

"It is absolutely mind-blowing when you think of what we are going to do."

Rosetta project manager, John Elwood

WORD STATION
Kuiper belt part of the solar system beyond the orbit of the planet Neptune

Ice dwarves of the Kuiper belt

As we have seen, many **comets** exist beyond the **orbit** of the planet Neptune. This area is called the **Kuiper belt**. The objects in this belt are called **Kuiper belt objects (KBOs)**. Some KBOs are huge.

Not even the powerful Hubble Space **Telescope** can capture a clear image of distant Pluto. The smaller object seen below here is Pluto's **moon**, Charon.

WORD STATION

dwarf planet large body orbiting the Sun that is smaller than major planets

Pluto

KUIPER BELT

Sun

Neptune

The icy objects in the Kuiper belt circle the solar system. They go beyond the orbit of Neptune.

Dwarf planets

In 2005 scientists announced that they had discovered an enormous KBO, called Eris. They wondered if they should call Eris a planet of the **solar system**. Instead, they created a new category for KBOs like Eris. They called them **dwarf planets**. This category would also include Pluto. Pluto had once been called the ninth planet in the solar system. Today, five dwarf planets are known: Ceres, Pluto, Haumea, Makemake, and Eris.

New Horizons

NASA's New Horizons space **probe** will visit Pluto in 2015. This will be the first time a probe from Earth has visited Pluto. After its visit with Pluto, New Horizons will continue on to investigate other KBOs.

"We're in the space exploration business and the outer solar system is a wild, woolly place. We haven't explored it very well."

Alan Stern

Solar Explorers

There would be no life on Earth without the Sun's heat and light. The rest of the **solar system** also needs the Sun. The Sun's powerful **gravity** holds everything else in place. Scientists are always eager to learn more about the Sun.

Genesis

NASA's Genesis **probe** was sent to capture material from the Sun. It went into the outer areas of the Sun's **atmosphere**. Then, a return capsule, holding samples, was sent back to Earth. Unfortunately, when the capsule returned to Earth, its parachutes did not open. It crashed into the ground at high speed. Luckily, some samples could still be used for research.

The Genesis return capsule crashed as it returned to Earth from the Sun. Still, scientists found some usable samples.

The STEREO B satellite took this image of the **Moon** passing in front of the Sun.

Seeing in STEREO

NASA's STEREO (Solar Terrestrial Relations Observatory) **mission** uses two **satellites**. These are being used to capture never-before-seen images of the Sun. One satellite travels ahead of Earth in its **orbit**. The other satellite follows behind. You might think of them as being like left and right eyes. They work together to build up a full image.

SOHO

SOHO (the Solar and Heliospheric Observatory) is a project run by several countries. Launched in 1995, it is run by the **ESA** and **NASA**. This **satellite** has been sending huge amounts of information about the Sun back to scientists on Earth.

This shows SOHO being assembled. The solar panels are flat against the sides at the bottom here. They opened out once SOHO reached space.

solar panels

CASE STUDY:

Saving SOHO

The SOHO **mission** almost came to a disastrous end in 1998. A mistake caused scientists on Earth to lose contact with the satellite. SOHO had gone into a spin. Its **solar panels** were not where they were supposed to be. This meant that the SOHO was not creating any power. The deep chill of outer space would freeze its batteries (power source) and fuel.

SOHO sent back never-before-seen images of the Sun. The colors here are created by computers. The Sun doesn't look blue in space!

After six weeks of silence, scientists picked up the first signals from SOHO. This was the first sign that it could receive commands from scientists on Earth again. Immediately the team began to try to regain control of the craft.

Return to life

Over the next three weeks, the batteries slowly recharged. They got power after being exposed to some sunlight. Eventually there was enough power to begin to thaw out some of SOHO's rocket engines. The team could then make tiny adjustments. Over nine days, they stopped SOHO's spin. They pointed it toward the Sun once more.

By the end of 1998, all of the **instruments** on board SOHO were working normally. Over 10 years later, SOHO is still helping scientists to understand how the Sun works.

Other Stars, Other Worlds

For centuries, people have wondered if there are other planets. In 1992 scientists used a **radio telescope** to discover two new planets. They were **orbiting** a distant star.

Since then, more than 490 **exoplanets** have been discovered. These are planets that orbit stars other than the Sun. In 1995 a planet was discovered that was between half and twice as big as the planet Jupiter. So far, all the discoveries have been of planets like this.

This exoplanet is so close to its star that it is being pulled apart by it.

WORD STATION
radio telescope instrument that picks up radio waves

Professor Sara Seager is a world expert on exoplanets. She works with the Kepler Space Telescope.

Spitzer surprises

In 2005 the Spitzer Space **Telescope** made an amazing discovery. It captured **infrared** light from two exoplanets. This was the first time light from planets beyond the **solar system** had been observed. Two years later, Spitzer found evidence of water on an exoplanet.

Flying in formation

NASA hopes to launch five spacecraft. They will work together as a single huge telescope. This telescope should pick up the distant light of an Earth-like planet.

The hunt for other Earths

The search is on to find Earth-like planets. A number of **missions** will join in the hunt. One of these is the Kepler Space Telescope, launched in 2009. Early results in 2010 showed that Kepler has indeed discovered many new planets.

The flecks of light in this Hubble Space Telescope image are not stars. They are incredibly distant galaxies. They each contain billions of stars.

WORD STATION
galaxy collection of billions of stars

The speed of light

The fastest thing in the **universe** is light. It speeds from the stars to Earth at 300,000 kilometers (186,000 miles) per second. But in space, light also has enormous distances to travel. It takes four years for light to make the trip from the *nearest* star, Proxima Centauri, to Earth.

Across the universe

Using a **telescope**, we can see things that are very distant in time. This is because we can study light that traveled in the very distant past. **Galaxies** are collections of billions of stars that are far off in the universe. Some galaxies are so far away that light left them 13 billion years ago. Studying this light can help scientists understand the galaxies' size, age, and history.

Aboard the Hubble Space Telescope is a very special camera. In 2009 scientists got some amazing images from this camera. These and similar images are providing more information about distant galaxies all the time.

Back to the beginning

Using these same ideas, scientists are learning about the age of the universe. Most scientists believe that the universe began as a tiny point. Then, billions of years ago, there was a big explosion. This is known as the **Big Bang**. After this explosion, the tiny point began to expand, or get bigger. Scientists believe the universe has been expanding ever since.

Scientists have measured slight **waves** of **energy** in space. They are left over from the Big Bang. These waves have allowed scientists to guess the age of the universe. Currently the universe is believed to be around 13.5 billion years old.

Being There

This volunteer prepares to spend 500 days in a space capsule. This will help scientists prepare for a real mission to Mars.

Most space scientists probably dream of being able to visit the stars and planets they study. What does the future hold for human travel into deep space, beyond the **Moon**?

The distant stars

The stars are so far away that we may never reach them. The **probe** Voyager 1, currently speeding from the **solar system** at over 60,000 kilometers (37,300 miles) per hour, would take around 75,000 years to reach the nearest star!

Mission to Mars

A trip to our nearest planet, Mars, would take over a year. In May 2010, six volunteers were locked away in a spacecraft. The plan is for them to stay there for over 500 days. They will see what a flight to Mars might be like. Their pretend spaceship includes a Mars **lander**. There is also an area that has been made to look like a landscape on Mars. Three of the crew members are scheduled to act out a Mars landing. All of this will help scientists plan a real **mission** to Mars someday. Some people think this real mission could take place around the 2030s.

Human explorers will perhaps visit the surface of Mars one day.

Humans versus robots

Humans pose problems for space exploration. Humans are big and heavy. They need food, water, and air to breathe. They need to be protected against **waves** of **energy** in space. And they want to come home again! All of this means having to build big, powerful rockets to boost everything needed into space. At the moment, it makes more sense to use **telescopes** and robot space probes. They do not eat, sleep, or get bored on long journeys. Plus they can travel to places where no human could survive.

Is there anyone out there?

Could our space **probes** send back proof of other living things in the **universe**?

Astrobiology is the study of life in the universe. **NASA's** Astrobiology Program looks for answers to these three major questions:

- How does life begin and develop?
- Is there life beyond Earth?
- If there is, how can we find it?

Experts in different kinds of science are involved in astrobiology. Several space **missions** play a part in astrobiology research. The Spitzer and Kepler **telescopes** hunt for Earth-like planets. The Mars **rovers** search for proof of life on Mars.

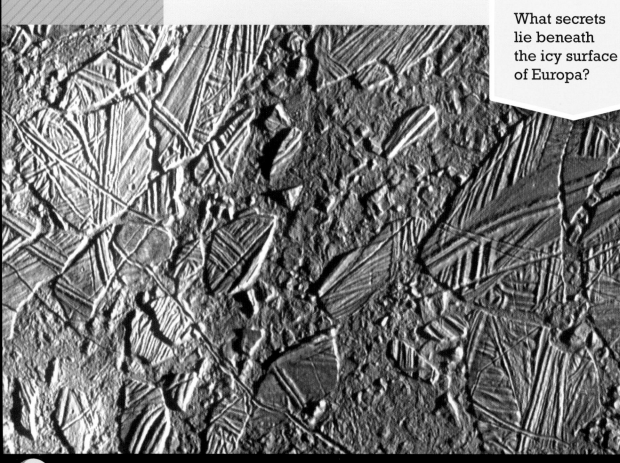

What secrets lie beneath the icy surface of Europa?

WORD STATION
astrobiology study of life in the universe

These are radio telescopes in the state of California. They are part of SETI's mission to pick up signals from space.

Europa

One of the planet Jupiter's largest **moons** is called Europa. Its surface is made of ice. Scientists believe that there may be an ocean of water underneath. Some scientists think that there may be life in that ocean. Finding out will be tricky. It will involve a journey to Europa. It will also involve drilling as much as 100 kilometers (62 miles) through the ice.

SETI

"SETI" stands for the "Search for Extraterrestrial Intelligence." This means the search for intelligent life outside of Earth. Scientists use **radio telescopes** to find evidence of signals from creatures beyond Earth. So far, the search has been unsuccessful. We have sent messages, but no one has answered . . . yet.

Still, there is no reason to believe that Earth is the only place in the universe where life has appeared. We have not found life elsewhere. Yet that does not mean that it is not there.

Timeline of Space Exploration

2296 BCE (about 4,300 years ago)	Chinese **astronomers** record that they have seen a **comet**.
270 BCE	Aristarchus says the Sun is bigger than Earth. He also says that Earth goes around it.
1609 CE	Galileo Galilei builds one of the first **telescopes**.
1655	Christiaan Huygens improves the design of the telescope.
1687	Isaac Newton explains his ideas about **gravity**.
1781	William Herschel discovers there are star systems beyond our **galaxy**.
1915	The star Proxima Centauri is discovered. It is the nearest star to Earth other than the Sun.
1932	Karl Jansky tells the world about **radio waves** in the **universe**.
1957	The Soviet Union launches the first **satellite**, Sputnik 1.
1957	Laika the dog becomes the first living creature to **orbit** Earth, aboard Sputnik 2.
1959	The space **probe** Luna 3 sends back the first images of the far side of the **Moon**.
1961	Yuri Gagarin of the Soviet Union becomes the first person to orbit Earth.
February 1966	Luna 9 makes the first controlled landing on the surface of the Moon.
1968	The crew of Apollo 8 are the first people from Earth to orbit the Moon.
1969	Apollo 11 **astronauts** Neil Armstrong and Edwin (Buzz) Aldrin are the first people to walk on the Moon.
1970	Venera 7 is the first probe to successfully land on the surface of Venus.
April 1971	Salyut 1 is launched. It is the first space station to orbit Earth.
November 1971	Mariner 9 reaches Mars. It becomes the first space probe from Earth to orbit another planet.
1972	Apollo 17 returns to Earth from the Moon.

1976	Viking 1 makes the first successful landing on Mars.
1980	Voyager 1 reaches Saturn. It sends back the first detailed pictures of the ringed planet.
1989	Voyager 2 sends back the first close-up images of the planet Neptune.
April 25, 1990	The Hubble Space Telescope is carried into orbit aboard the space shuttle Discovery.
1992	**NASA** launches SETI, the Search for Extraterrestrial Intelligence.
1997	The remote-controlled Sojourner **rover** travels on Mars.
2000	The first crew begins working aboard the International Space Station.
2005	The Huygens space probe lands on the surface of Titan, one of the moons of Saturn.
January 2006	Samples from the Stardust **mission** to Comet Wild 2 reach Earth.
October 2006	The twin STEREO space probes launch to study the Sun.
*2011	MESSENGER is due to enter orbit around Mercury.
2014	Rosetta is due to meet up with a comet.
2015	New Horizon will make a flyby of Pluto and the **Kuiper belt**.
2020	India and Japan plan landings on the Moon with astronauts.

* Dates in 2011 and beyond are planned, but are subject to change.

Glossary

asteroid rocky object orbiting the Sun in the solar system. Asteroids vary greatly in size.

astrobiology study of life in the universe

astronaut person who travels to space in a spacecraft

astronomer scientist who studies space and everything in it

astronomy scientific study of space

atmosphere layer of gases that surrounds a planet

base permanent location that can be used over time

Big Bang idea that the universe started with a tiny point about 13.5 billion years ago, and has been expanding ever since

comet fairly small, icy object that orbits the Sun. When a comet approaches the Sun, it produces a long tail of gas and dust.

constellation pattern of stars in the night sky

dark energy mysterious source of energy that explains why the universe is expanding more rapidly

dark matter invisible material that forms most of a galaxy

dwarf planet large body in space that orbits the Sun, but is not large enough to be classified in the same group as the major planets

electromagnetic spectrum range of waves of energy that travel through space

energy ability to do work

European Space Agency (ESA) group of 18 European nations that work together to study space

exoplanet planet outside the solar system that orbits a star other than the Sun

galaxy collection of billions of stars

gamma describes waves of energy that travel through space that are short, very high energy, and mostly taken in by the atmosphere

gas substance with no definite shape, like air

gravity pull that a large object has on a smaller one nearby

gravity assist using the gravity of a planet to change the speed and flight path of a space probe

infrared describes waves of energy that travel through space. We feel them as heat.

instrument piece of equipment used to perform a certain task

Kuiper belt part of the solar system beyond the orbit of the planet Neptune, occupied by millions of comets and dwarf planets

Kuiper belt object (KBO) comet or dwarf planet that exists beyond the orbit of Neptune

lander space vehicle that lands on the surface of an object in space, such as a planet or moon

launcher vehicle that carries something, such as a satellite, into space

meteorite space rock that crashes onto the surface of another larger object in space, such as a moon or planet

mission space program or flight with a specific goal

moon small natural object made of rock that orbits a planet

National Aeronautics and Space Administration (NASA) U.S. space agency

orbit circle around something, such as a planet

probe spacecraft that carries instruments for research, but not astronauts

radio describes the longest type of energy wave that travels through space

radio telescope device that picks up radio waves, to see objects in regions of space where visible light cannot pass through

rover vehicle that travels across a planet's surface

satellite object that orbits, or circles around, a planet

solar panel instrument that converts the Sun's light energy into electricity

solar system our Sun and its family of planets, asteroids, and other objects that orbit it

Southern Equatorial Belt group of clouds circling around the planet Jupiter

telescope instrument that makes distant objects, such as planets and stars, appear much nearer and bigger

universe all of space and everything in it

wave invisible path of movement followed by forms of energy

X-ray describes waves of energy that travel through space that are short, very high energy, and mostly absorbed by the atmosphere

Find Out More

Books

Dowswell, Paul. *First Encyclopedia of Space.* Tulsa, Okla.: EDC, 2010.

Harrison, Paul. *Up Close: Space.* New York: Rosen, 2008.

Parker, Steve. *How It Works: Space Exploration.* Broomall, Pa.: Mason Crest, 2011.

Schneider, Howard. *Backyard Guide to the Night Sky.* Washington, D.C.: National Geographic, 2009.

Websites

www.nasa.gov
Visit the website of NASA, an excellent starting-off point for information on all aspects of space exploration.

www.esa.int/esaCP/index.html
Visit the website of the ESA to learn more about its missions.

www.newton.dep.anl.gov/askasci/astron98.htm
This Argonne National Laboratory website answers hundreds of questions about astronomy.

http://hubblesite.org
The Hubble Space Telescope website offers the latest news and findings, as well as links to a wealth of information on astronomy.

www.iwaswondering.org/heidi_homepage.html
Check out space scientist Heidi Hammel's kid-friendly guide to space exploration.

www.skyandtelescope.com
Visit the website of *Sky and Telescope*, a magazine for amateur astronomers.

Places to visit

Smithsonian National Air and Space Museum

Independence Ave at 6th Street, SW
Washington, D.C. 20560
www.nasm.si.edu

This museum is full of examples of technology and photos from the history of space flight.

John F. Kennedy Space Center

Kennedy Space Center, Florida 32899
www.kennedyspacecenter.com

While visiting the Kennedy Space Center, you may be able to witness the launch of a spacecraft.

Index

Akatsuki space probe 18–19
Apollo missions 14
Aristarchus (astronomer) 5
asteroids 15, 17, 20
astrobiology 40, 41
astronauts 14, 15, 38, 39
astronomers 5, 6–7, 10, 11, 24, 32, 40
atmospheres 7, 8, 9, 11, 19, 23, 28

Big Bang 35
brown dwarf stars 10

carbon dioxide 19
Chandra X-ray Observatory 37
China 5, 15
comets 9, 24, 25
constellations 5

dark energy 36, 37
Discovery (space shuttle) 9
dwarf planets 26, 27

electromagnetic spectrum 10, 11
Elwood, John 25
Europa (moon) 41
European Space Agency 19, 24, 30
exoplanets 32, 33

galaxies 10, 35, 36, 37
Galilei, Galileo 6–7, 41
gamma rays 11
Genesis space probe 28–29
gravity 23, 28, 36, 37
gravity assist 16, 17, 24
Greece 5

Hammel, Heidi 9
Hazcams (hazard cameras) 21
Hubble Space Telescope 8, 9, 35
India 5, 15
infrared waves 11, 19, 33

James Webb Space Telescope 9
Japan 15, 18
Juno space probe 23
Jupiter 7, 9, 13, 22, 23, 41

Kepler Space Telescope 33, 40
Kuiper belt objects (KBOs) 24, 26, 27
Kuiper, Gerard 24

life 6, 14, 20, 28, 40, 41
light 7, 9, 10, 11, 13, 28, 31, 33, 35, 36
Lowell, Percival 6

Mariner space probes 6, 13, 16
Mars 6, 20, 21, 24, 39, 40
Mercury 16, 17, 19
Mercury Dual Imaging System (MDIS) 17
MESSENGER satellite 17
meteorites 15
Moon 5, 6, 10, 14–15, 20, 29
moons 7, 10, 12, 13, 20, 41

NASA 23, 30, 31, 33, 37, 40
Neptune 24
New Horizons space probe 26, 27

Opportunity rover 20, 21
Orton, Glenn 22

planetary scientists 12, 13, 22, 40
Pluto (dwarf planet) 26, 27

radiation 11, 24, 35, 39
radio telescopes 10, 32, 41
radio waves 10, 21
Rosetta space probe 24, 25
rovers 20, 21, 40

satellites 11, 17, 18, 19, 29, 31, 37
Saturn 13, 20
SETI (Search for Extraterrestrial Intelligence) 41
SOHO (Solar and Heliospheric Observatory) 30, 31
Southern Equatorial Belt (SEB) 22, 23
space probes 6, 12, 13, 15, 16, 18–19, 20, 21, 23, 24, 25, 26, 27, 28–29, 30, 38, 39, 40

Spirit rover 20, 21
Spitzer Space Telescope 10, 11, 33, 35, 40
stars 5, 10, 11, 28, 30, 31, 32, 33, 35, 38, 41
STEREO (Solar Terrestrial Relations Observatory) 29
Student Dust Counter (SDC) 26
Sun 5, 6, 10, 11, 16, 19, 24, 28, 29, 30, 31

telescopes 6–7, 8, 9, 10, 11, 12, 14, 32, 33, 35, 39, 40, 41
temperatures 10, 11, 19, 33
Titan (moon) 20

universe 6, 7, 9, 11, 35, 36, 37, 41

Venus 13, 16, 17, 18–19, 20
Venus Express space probe 19
Voyager 1 space probe 13, 38

weather 18, 29
Wide Field Camera 3 (WFC3) 35
winds 18–19, 22

X-rays 11, 37